NASCAR Fan Experience

Matt Doeden
AR B.L.: 2.6
Points: 0.5   MG

The World of NASCAR

NASCAR Fan Experience

by Matt Doeden

Reading Consultant:
Barbara J. Fox
Reading Specialist
North Carolina State University

Content Consultant:
Betty L. Carlan
Research Librarian
International Motorsports Hall of Fame
Talladega, Alabama

Capstone
press

Mankato, Minnesota

Blazers is published by Capstone Press,
151 Good Counsel Drive, P.O. Box 669, Mankato, Minnesota 56002.
www.capstonepress.com

Library of Congress Cataloging-in-Publication Data
Doeden, Matt.
    NASCAR fan experience / by Matt Doeden.
    p. cm. — (Blazers. The World of NASCAR)
    Includes bibliographical references and index.
    ISBN-13: 978-1-4296-1282-1 (hardcover)
    ISBN-10: 1-4296-1282-7 (hardcover)
    1. Stock car racing — United States — Juvenile literature. 2. NASCAR
(Association) — Juvenile literature. I. Title. II. Series.
GV1029.9.S74D636 2008
796.72 — dc22   2007027426

Summary: Describes what NASCAR fans can experience at live racing events,
including before, during, and after the race.

Essential content terms are **bold** and are defined on the spread where they
first appear.

Editorial Credits
Tom Adamson & Mandy Robbins, editors; Bobbi J. Wyss, designer;
    Jo Miller, photo researcher

Photo Credits
AP Images/Alan Marler, 20–21; Chuck Burton, 10; Gene Blythe, 14–15;
    Steve Helber, 5, 24
Corbis/Reuters/Pierre Ducharme, 26–27; The Sharpe Image/Sam Sharpe, 22
DVIC/SRA Brian Ferguson, USAF, 7
Getty Images for NASCAR/Chris Trotman, 6; Rusty Jarrett, cover, 25; Getty
    Images, Inc./Gilles Mingasson, 17; Harry How, 12–13; Rusty Jarrett, 19
The Sharpe Image/Sam Sharpe, 18, 28, 29
ZUMA Press/Rusty Burroughs/TSN, 8–9

1 2 3 4 5 6 13 12 11 10 09 08

Table of Contents

At the Track 4

Before the Race 11

Race Day 16

The Race Is On! 23

Bristol Motor Speedway diagram 20

Glossary 30

Read More 31

Internet Sites 31

Index 32

At the Track

The **grandstands** are packed. Most fans wear the colors of their favorite NASCAR drivers. Some fans hold up signs. Others munch on snacks.

grandstand — the main area at a racetrack where the fans sit

Fans cheer and boo during driver introductions. They remove their hats for the national anthem. Air Force jets soar overhead before the race.

Casey Mears

Finally, the big moment arrives.
The green flag waves. Stock cars roar
down the track.

TRACK FACT!

Get comfortable. NASCAR races last three to four hours, sometimes longer.

Before the Race

NASCAR races are huge events. Hundreds of thousands of fans flock to speedways. Many fans spend the weekend camping at the track.

There is plenty of action to see before the race. Fans can go to practice sessions. They watch **qualifying** laps. The race's starting order is decided during qualifying.

qualifying — the process by which teams earn a starting spot in a race

TRACK FACT!

The final practice before the big race is called Happy Hour. Race teams use it to make final adjustments to their cars.

Fans soak in the NASCAR experience.
They buy **souvenirs**. They try to meet
their favorite drivers and get autographs.

souvenir — something people keep
to remind them of an experience

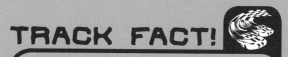

TRACK FACT!

With a garage pass, fans can visit the race teams and see the cars up close.

Race Day

The excitement peaks on race day. Fans come to the track early. Some barbecue in the parking lot. Others eat at the track's many **concession stands**.

concession stand — a place where fans can buy food and drinks

TRACK FACT!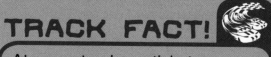

At some tracks, a ticket can cost $150 or more.

Most fans watch the long ceremony before the race. The ceremony ends with the most famous words in racing: "Gentlemen, start your engines!"

hitting the start switch

TRACK FACT!

Usually, someone famous gets the honor of saying, "Gentlemen, start your engines!"

19

Bristol Motor Speedway

scoring pylon

haulers

victory circle

pit road

grandstands

21

The Race Is On!

Everyone jumps to their feet as the green flag waves. Fans cheer for exciting passes. They gasp as cars spin wildly out of control.

Drivers and their crews talk to each other with radios. Fans can use radios to listen to them talk about race **strategy**.

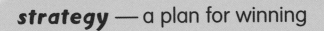

strategy — a plan for winning

TRACK FACT!

Most tracks have a scoring pylon. This tower lists the running order of the cars.

25

It's a close race. The leaders fight for the checkered flag. The fans go crazy!

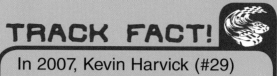

TRACK FACT!

In 2007, Kevin Harvick (#29) won the Daytona 500 by only .02 seconds.

The fun isn't over. The winner thrills
fans with a burnout or a victory lap. Fans
stay at the track to watch the winner in
victory circle. They enjoy every moment.

Matt Kenseth

Glossary

anthem (AN-thuhm) — a national song

burnout (BURN-owt) — a cloud of smoke created when a driver spins the tires, to celebrate a victory

concession stand (kuhn-SESH-uhn STAND) — a booth where people can buy food and drinks

grandstand (GRAND-stand) — the main area at a racetrack with seats for fans

qualifying (KWAHL-uh-fye-ing) — how drivers earn a starting spot in a race; each driver gets two qualifying laps to post the best possible time.

souvenir (soo-vuh-NIHR) — an object that a person keeps to remind him or her of a place, person, or event

strategy (STRAT-uh-gee) — a plan to win

Read More

Cavin, Curt. *Race Day: The Fastest Show on Earth.* The World of NASCAR. Excelsior, Minn.: Tradition Books, 2003.

Doeden, Matt. *At the Races.* NASCAR Racing. Mankato, Minn.: Capstone Press, 2008.

Eagen, Rachel. *NASCAR.* Automania! New York: Crabtree, 2007.

Internet Sites

FactHound offers a safe, fun way to find Internet sites related to this book. All of the sites on FactHound have been researched by our staff.

Here's how:
1. Visit *www.facthound.com*
2. Choose your grade level.
3. Type in this book ID **1429612827** for age-appropriate sites. You may also browse subjects by clicking on letters, or by clicking on pictures or words.
4. Click on the **Fetch It** button.

FactHound will fetch the best sites for you!

Index

autographs, 14

burnouts, 28

camping, 11
cars, 8, 13, 15, 23, 25
ceremonies, 18
checkered flags, 26
concession stands, 16

Daytona 500, 27
drivers, 4, 6, 14, 24, 27

food, 4, 16

garage passes, 15
grandstands, 4
green flags, 8, 23

Happy Hour, 13
Harvick, Kevin, 27

national anthem, 6

practicing, 12, 13

qualifying, 12

race weekends, 11
radios, 24

souvenirs, 14

tickets, 17

victory circle, 28

winners, 27, 28